Praise for Nesting for Empty Nesters®

"Francisca Alonso has created a very useful tool with her new book Nesting for Empty Nesters®. If the thoughtful advice and the provocative questions don't get you thinking down the right track, the inspiring photography will certainly have you itching to build the home of your dreams."

Kevin Daum, Inc.
Columnist and Author of *Building your Own Home For Dummies*

"Like Dorothy in the Wizard of Oz, many of us realize, 'There's no place like home.' One quick read of Nesting for Empty Nesters® by Francisca Alonso was enough to make me begin to re-imagine my future in the community and with the amenities I have grown to love. Why not renovate an existing property to meet the next stage of life? This fantastic step-by-step guide will help you evaluate whether the age-in-place vacation lifestyle is right for you. Well done!"

Lisa Lipkind Leibow
Client and Author of *Double Out and Back*

"Their consultative approach helped take my small idea and expand upon it to design my vacation style home. Now that I have experienced their process I can see the value of the ideas in this book for any person who wants to build their aging-in-place home or remodel their existing home. Reading this book will help you create your vision and Francisca and Tony will help you fill in the gaps. Read the book and begin dreaming about your Vacation Style home."

Gordon J. Bernhardt
Client and President & CEO, Bernhardt Wealth Management, Inc.

Client Testimonials

"We changed the whole feel and flow of our home with the addition of an 8 foot hallway and kitchen renovation. The addition of the hallway allowed us to open up the back of the house letting light in and incorporating outdoor living space to our home. We were very pleased with the entire process from start to finish. Francisca was wonderful to work with. How many people can say that their architect builder became their good friend....we can."

   - Louise and Ted, Clients

"AV Architects + Builders designed and built a two story addition to our home, including a new family room, breakfast room, and re-designing our existing family room into a mudroom and kid's study downstairs; and a new master bedroom, and re-designing the existing master bedroom into two walk-in closets, sitting room, and upstairs laundry room. This addition improved our storage, and the flow of our home tremendously. It made it perfect for a family with three growing boys and two big dogs. Having the architect manage the project from beginning to end was a huge benefit. This made for a very responsive contractor, who stayed on top of the job from start to finish."

   - Lisa and Phil, Clients

"We just finished a kitchen renovation with AV Architects and Builders and I can't say enough about the gorgeous job they did. Francisca was AMAZING! She helped bring everything together from the back splash to the granite island and new tile floor. She was so easy to work with, she really took into consideration my floor plan, taste and daily living patterns and it is all reflected in the materials and their quality, not to mention her fabulous taste. The job was also scheduled, and completed earlier than expected; her staff is very prompt and efficient. This job was so well organized and her company left nothing undone. Francisca has a great eye for building and renovating and we will definitely use her in the future for more projects."

   - Liz and Don, Clients

"We hired AV Architects + Builders to expand and update our 1980 brick colonial. The project consisted of a complete renovation and reconfiguration of the kitchen and 3 baths, the relocation of a laundry room, the construction of a mudroom and a 2-level addition including a bathroom suite on the upper level. We thoroughly enjoyed working with Francisca and her team at AV. Francisca is familiar with current trends, but also considers the efficiency and effectiveness of the natural flow within a house. The contractors at AV were all professional and considerate. Our concerns with such a large project were budget and timeliness. We were pleasantly surprised and pleased that we were able to move back into our "new" home on time and without any budget overruns. We are 100% happy with the work AV has done in our home and highly recommend the team."

   - Nora and Gray, Clients

We selected AV Architects + Builders to create a new kitchen in our 1954 New England Salt Box home in Northern Virginia. We interviewed four firms, but selected AV because they understood us better than anyone. We wanted a firm that could create a completely new kitchen that replaced the existing small kitchen and one car garage, but could do so within a reasonable budget and still achieve a combination of an updated modern space that would blend with the traditional character of the house. They achieved our dream within the expected time frame. We love our new kitchen and we are enjoying every piece in it, which was chosen with their guidance and expertise. We were very lucky to find a firm who could combine the architectural design, the contracting and the development of the project. The combination made all the process smoother. Francisca, Tony and their entire crew made all this project easy by working closely with us. Our best experience with them was finding our countertops, which we love but were tough to find because we wanted something very specific. Francisca was excellent at interpreting my ideas and making them real."

- Larisa and Lock, Clients

"My fiancé and I met with Francisca and Tony after we got engaged to discuss rebuilding on our property. The 800 sq. ft. brick house I owned wasn't going to be big enough for our 3 dogs and us! The design phase was a lot of fun and very detailed, but never overwhelming. We went away to get married the same week our house was demo'd and 8 short months later were back on our property in our dream home!! What I love most about the house is the kitchen, the stairwell, the windows, the mudroom, and the dog-wash station in the mudroom... I love it all. Francisca and Tony think of all the little things that add so much detail and really make a home feel finished. If I ever build another home I know whom to call!"

- Mey and Brandon, Clients

"It was a great pleasure working with AV Architects + Builders on my kitchen renovation project. Francisca spent quality time with me during the planning phases of the project to ensure that I came up with the best possible design for our kitchen. She guided me through the selection process of cabinets, appliances, light fixtures, tiles, and paint colors. It was definitely a collaboration where she took my ideas and feedback and ran with them as well as adding design concepts I never would have thought of. She also was a great project manager and managed the workers to make sure the workmanship was up to her high standards. Quality is a key requirement for AV Architects and they insist on using products and materials that will last. The result is that my kitchen looks as good today as the day it was completed."

- Amy and Martin, Clients

"We were very fortunate to use AV Architects + Builders to handle our kitchen, mud room and bath remodel. Francisca's designs were perfect, both functional and elegant. She completed the work on time and within budget. We truly appreciate that she was with us every step of the journey; both in our home and in every store we visited. Francisca not only helped create our vision, but also delivered it flawlessly. AV Architects is a great company. We plan to be lifelong customers and consider them a part of our family."

- Bill and Michelle, Clients

"We have completed two significant projects with AV Architects + Builders and have been extremely satisfied. They redesigned and built our kitchen and master bath several years back. More recently they finished redesigning and building our family room, children's lounge and basement. Both projects were completed on time and were delivered as promised."

- Chris and Lauren, Clients

"I hired AV Architects + Builders to do a total renovation of my home in Vienna, VA. An addition to my home, total kitchen and bathroom redesign, deck and exterior redesign. Ten years later, I can say I have never had an issue with their work, solid construction and everything still looks brand new. In fact, I am about to hire them again for another project. They are creative, understand client needs and budget. THE BEST."

- Dolores, Client

"AV Architects + Builders provided an innovative solution to our remodeling needs. They were far more engaged with us than other companies who gave us designs and estimates. We met all our design objectives within the budget we set for the project. The construction phase stayed on time. AV Architects addressed all issues in a timely fashion. We would definitely engage them for future remodeling needs."

- Mary and Ed, Clients

"Very professional design team that dealt with numerous challenges to existing house modifications and small guesthouse, in particular with dealing with permitting and zoning issues, and keeping homeowner informed."

- Arden and Tony, Clients

"AV Architects + Builders did a complete renovation of my home. They were totally professional and the project turned out beautiful. What I appreciated the most is that they took care of every detail. We just love the finished project and take great pride in showing it off."

- Beverly, Client

"Finding the right architect is never an easy process, but when we met AV Architects + Builders our problems were solved. They helped us visualize the potential of our home and helped us stay within our budget. AV Architects + Builders are true Solution Builders."

- Patricia and Wilco, Clients

Nesting for Empty Nesters® :

The Vacation Style Living™ Approach to Aging in Place

Nesting for Empty Nesters®:
The Vacation Style Living™ Approach to Aging in Place

The practical guide to using smart design to prepare your home now
for a better quality of life in retirement and beyond

by
Francisca Alonso, Assoc. AIA
Certified Aging in Place Specialist (CAPS)

with Antonio Alonso, AIA

Co-Founders of AV Architects + Builders
Great Falls, Virginia

Cover Photo: Stacy Zarin Goldberg Photography
Architect/Builder: Francisca and Antonio Alonso

Cover Design & Book Layout: Michael Spillane

Published by

Nesting for Empty Nesters®: The Vacation Style Living™ Approach to Aging in Place
ISBN: 978-0-9972922-2-0

Acknowledgements

I believe we are a combination of the people in our lives that inspire us. They all motivate us and enhance our lives in different ways. All of those influences have not only shaped my life, they are also reflected in the work that I do and love, and so they are a part of this book.

To my husband Tony for always being my biggest fan and being willing to try every crazy design and business idea that I have. For always being up for the next idea – to experiment, to try, to push the envelope – and above all, to be myself. He is my stability.

To our four children, Lucas, Sofia, Marcus and Julian, who remind me every day of what really matters. They keep my feet on the ground and keep me going at the same time.

To my father Melvin Villarroel for showing me that you should love your job and make a difference with that privilege. "I love what I do and I get paid for it too, can you believe it?" he would say. He loved what he did so much that all three of my siblings and I became architects. He took his work very seriously and believed that architecture is for the benefit of humankind and that it should not be taken lightly. To his last day he loved his work and had an incredible passion for it.

To my mom Antje Villarroel for giving me an amazing work ethic and for showing us how important family is. As a stay-at-home mom, she never stopped working hard for our family. She sewed our clothes when we were kids, raised us and did everything that she could to support my father in growing his business. To this day she goes above and beyond to help anyone that needs a hand.

In life, I wanted a piece of my mom's life and a piece of my dad's life. I have both now and I am immensely grateful for their example, their love, and their guidance.

To my siblings Pablo, Matias, and my sister Antonia, for being my college roommates, my colleagues, my mentors, and my collaborators. There is nothing like their unconditional love and support.

To my mother-in-law Rosa Alonso for being a wonderful grandma to my children. She is a big part of our success. She would happily watch the children – even when they were 6 months old, 2, 3, and 4 years old. When we were starting to grow our business, she helped to grow our family, no questions asked.

To my editor and good friend Brigette Polmar who told me a year ago that we were going to write a book together. It seemed intangible and impossible at the time, but she made it happen.

And, of course, to all of our clients and friends who have always supported and encouraged us. Thank you for trusting us to help you reimagine your nests!

Photo Credit: Ali Rizvi Photography

INTRODUCTION
A Letter from the Author, Francisca Alonso

In designing, building and remodeling homes for countless families over many years, I have learned that designing or remodeling a home is a very personal process and unique every time. I've come to know what people like, what they don't, what they want and what they need – even when they sometimes aren't sure themselves. Smart design has to start with a family first and a clear understanding of how that family functions, only then can the design process begin. The same is true for aging in place and I have developed a deep passion for using smart design to create a high quality of life for my clients as they transition from being bustling families with young children to empty nesters and, ultimately, to retirees starting one of the greatest chapters of life. My goal is to provide empty nesters with a simplified lifestyle, a beautiful vacation-like retreat, and an easy to navigate space, so that they can enjoy these special years, welcome their families and explore new activities and passions. I call my approach Vacation Style Living™ because I incorporate the needs of the whole family to give them the lifestyle and quality of life they deserve at every stage of life. The following pages are illustrated with images of some of the Vacation Style Living™ homes I have created. I hope they will help you find inspiration as you prepare to reimagine your nest.

Photo Credit: Julian Alonso

I dedicate this book to my husband Antonio Alonso, my co-author, business partner and partner in life for more than 25 years. Thank you, Tony, for always being my biggest fan. I will always be yours...even when our nest is empty. Let the Vacation Style Living™ continue!

Wishing you all the very best nest,

Francisca Alonso

TABLE OF CONTENTS

Section 1: Aging in Place

Chapter 1   - Is Your Home Ready for the Next Stage of Your Life?

Chapter 2   - You Don't Need a Retirement Home –
             You Need a Great Home for Retirement

Chapter 3   - What is Aging in Place?

Chapter 4   - Right Where You Want to Be:
             Keeping Your Community and Reinventing Your Home

Chapter 5   - It's Decision Making Time: Choose Wisely

Chapter 6   - Does Your Home Serve Your Needs?

Chapter 7   - 10 Questions to Ask Yourself Now

Chapter 8   - Changing Needs, Smarter Design, Better Lifestyle

Chapter 9   - Do I Remodel, Move or Build New?

Chapter 10   - Building New for the New You – Considerations

Chapter 11   - Remodeling for Retirement and Beyond

Chapter 12   - Multi-Generational Living – Making Room for Mom & Dad

Chapter 13   - "I just can't see it." – When to Call in an Expert

Photo Credit: Stacy Zarin Goldberg Photography

Section 2: The Vacation Style Living™ Solution to Aging in Place

Chapter 14 - What is Vacation Style Living™?

Chapter 15 - What will I need?
The Elements of a Vacation Style Living™ Home for Retirement

Chapter 16 - Main Floor Living

Chapter 17 - Smarter Spaces: Where do you really "live"?

Chapter 18 - Finding Space and Maximizing Floor Plan

Chapter 19 - Does Size Really Matter? A New Approach to Square Footage

Chapter 20 - Vacation Style Living™ – The Basics of Vacation-Style Aging in Place

Chapter 21 - Find Inspiration

Chapter 22 - Choose a Style

Chapter 23 - Lighting

Chapter 24 - Interior Finishes

Chapter 25 - Hidden Hazards and Beautiful Solutions

Chapter 26 - Furniture

Chapter 27 - Elements to Eliminate

Chapter 28 - It's All About the Flow – Connecting Inside with Outside

Chapter 29 - Outdoor Spaces

Chapter 30 - Exterior Finishes

Section 3: Getting Started

Chapter 31   - Choosing an Architect

Chapter 32   - What is an Architect-Builder?

Chapter 33   - Interviewing Your Architect-Builder

Chapter 34   - Budgeting: How to Age in Place without Breaking the Bank

Chapter 35   - Start Now

About the Author – Francisca Alonso

About the Author – Antonio Alonso

Resources

Aging in Place

CHAPTER 1
Is Your Home Ready for the Next Stage of Your Life?

> ❝ Life is a balance of holding on and letting go. ❞
> – Rumi

Whether you're preparing for the day when your nest is empty or your chicks have already flown the coop, one thing is for certain; life is constantly changing. The question is: Is your house changing with you? Perhaps you've raised your children in your existing home or maybe you've already downsized once and are contemplating yet another transition. Wherever you are on your journey, if you plan well, the best may be yet to come – and we believe your best starts with your nest. As we begin to look at the art of using smart design now to ensure a better quality of life later – and longer - stop and take a good look around your home. Ask yourself: Is your home, as it is today, the comfortable, stylish retreat you need to really enjoy the next stage of your life? Is it a place friends and family long to visit, stay awhile and spend time with you? And, most importantly, is your home designed to make your everyday life easier, more convenient and more enjoyable 10, 20, even 30 years from now? The reality is, it can be and we can show you how. The secret is the Vacation Style Living™ approach to aging in place - the wise homeowner's strategy to living a long and active life in the home of your dreams and in the neighborhood you love.

 TIP: *One example of smart design is Universal Design. Universal Design is the design of homes to be safer, easier to use, more comfortable and more usable by most people. When updating your home look for Universal Design fixtures, finishes and features.*

CHAPTER 2

You Don't Need a Retirement Home – You Need a Great Home for Retirement

> ❝ Don't simply retire from something; have something to retire to. ❞
> – Henry Emerson Fosdick

Today, retirement isn't the end of an era. It's the beginning of a grand new adventure. An adventure filled with new interests, new hobbies, and maybe even new businesses. With innovations in smart home design and new products hitting the market every day designed to make your life as beautiful as it is convenient, people are staying at home – aging in place – longer and living life better than ever before. The fact is, today you don't need a retirement home. You need a great home for retirement. A home designed around your new lifestyle, that meets your needs inside and out, could help you stay in your own home into your 70s, 80s and beyond. But building your dream home – or remodeling your existing home into the house of your dreams – takes careful planning, wise budgeting and expert input. Why wait until it's too late? With the Vacation Style Living™ approach to aging in place, you can start designing your future today. Remember, your next stage could be your best stage. Make sure your home is ready to take you there.

 TIP: *According to the National Association of Home Builders, as many as 90% of homeowners will procrastinate in preparing their home for aging in place and risk being forced into last minute, potentially limited and costly, decisions by a health issue. Be one of the 10% - the planners – who anticipate their changing needs, or those of a family member, and proactively create the home of their dreams for retirement.*

CHAPTER 3

What is Aging in Place?

> 66 The ache for home lives in all of us, the safe place where we can go as we are and not be questioned. 99
> - Maya Angelou

Aging in place is living an active, fulfilling life, independently in your own home custom designed for your comfort, convenience and safety in retirement and beyond.

The Baby Boomers are transforming aging as we know it and as we speak. They are redefining retirement, reimagining their lives and remodeling their homes to support this new vision of the Golden Years. Boomers are healthier, more affluent and more productive than ever. They've raised their children, mastered their first – and maybe their second – careers, and are entering retirement with new goals, new activities and new passions to pursue. They want – and deserve – homes that give them the freedom to flourish into the future. They want homes that are beautiful, functional, open, welcoming, convenient and easy to navigate. Maybe for the first time, they can create the home they truly want, the home that's all about them, transforming their empty nest into the luxurious retreat they've always wanted. And then they want to stay there. Baby Boomers want to age in place.

 TIP: Baby Boomers are success focused. Consider the new trend of "successful aging." According to a recent AARP study people age 50+ who acknowledge their home may not be able to meet their physical needs as they get older, are likely to score lower when it comes to "successful aging." Designing your home for the next stage of life can put you in the aging winner's circle by helping you remain in your home longer and avoid costlier, less appealing options like assisted living and nursing homes.

Photo Credit: Stacy Zarin Goldberg Photography

CHAPTER 4

Right Where You Want to Be:
Keeping Your Community and Reinventing Your Home

> **"** Where you invest your love, you invest your life. **"**
>
> - Mumford & Sons

According to an AARP survey, among people age 50 to 64, nearly three-quarters, or 71%, want to age in place. But that number skyrockets by age 65, when AARP reports that 87% of adults want to stay in their current home and community as they age. In other words, most of us want to stay right where we are as long as we comfortably and safely can. Part of the convenience and comfort of aging in place within your existing community is knowing your surroundings, the amenities, cultural experiences, outdoor activities and the people that have become a part of your life. And while you may want to keep your community, you can still reinvent your home to meet your needs. As your nest empties and throughout retirement your life will change. Your home can – and should – change with you.

 TIP: *Updating your home to create a simplified, vacation-like lifestyle not only improves your quality of life, it can increase the value of your home. If you already love your neighborhood, learn to love your home again by transforming it into the oasis you deserve.*

Photo Credit: Stacy Zarin Goldberg Photography

CHAPTER 5
It's Decision Making Time: Choose Wisely

> **"You are never too old to set another goal or to dream a new dream."**
> - C.S. Lewis

As we've seen, most people as they approach retirement want to age in place, still few believe they need to start preparing for it. Vitality and an active lifestyle can fuel your passion for creating your personal oasis, or it can lull you into putting your planning on hold – a dangerous situation that can limit your choices down the road and stand between you and living your best life. Creating the perfect home for retirement and beyond will require several key decisions and can take several forms. You can move. You can stay. You can build a new house. You can buy another house. You can remodel the house you have. But one thing is clear: the earlier you decide where you're going to live, how you want to live and how you're going to get there, the easier and more successful the process will be. As you start to dream a new dream for your future, also start taking the first steps down the road to your new and improved lifestyle. Research, ask questions, discuss your desires and know your options, so you can make an informed and timely decision about what aging in place will look like for you.

 TIP: Who knows you better than you know yourself? Your spouse? A sibling or close friend? Maybe even a trusted physician, counselor or financial advisor? When making the important decision about how you will prepare your home to age in place, consult other key decision makers in your life. They may suggest aspects you haven't thought of or didn't realize were important. Their input can be priceless when working with your professional architect to remodel or build your home for retirement.

Photo Credit: Stacy Zarin Goldberg Photography

CHAPTER 6

Does Your Home Serve Your Needs?

> " Designing a home is about giving people spaces to live
> and allowing them an outlet to express themselves. "
>
> - Tripp Haenisch

Have you ever considered if your home really serves your needs? Many times we choose our homes based on their location, proximity to family, work, or good schools and neighborhoods. You may have chosen your house based on a certain budget, a specific number of bedrooms or to quickly prepare for a rapidly growing family. But now that you've lived in that house, maybe in several houses over time, you can start to assess with a keen and experienced eye how your house has – or hasn't – really met your needs. Any home – even a home we love – has its flaws. Look around your home and start to see where the layout, flow, size and distribution of square footage have made your life easier – and also notice where you've had to compromise or work a little harder to accomplish what you want within the space you live. Having a good understanding of what has helped you and what has hindered you in your home will go a long way to ensuring your new nest will serve you best.

 TIP: Don't forget about your guests. You're not just preparing your home for your retirement, but also for those who will be enjoying it with you! "Visitability" – the ability for guests to easily access the main level of your home – takes into consideration things like a main floor powder room, wide and step-free entrances, and curb appeal to make these easy-to-access homes easy on the eyes, as well.

Photo Credit: Stacy Zarin Goldberg Photography

CHAPTER 7
10 Questions to Ask Yourself Now

> " Architecture is the thoughtful making of space. "
> – Louis Khan

Really "seeing" your home and how it may or may not serve your needs today and in the future can be difficult. The following questions may help you see where you can improve your home for aging in place.

1. When you entertain, do you have enough room for guests to sit and interact comfortably?

2. Does your kitchen allow you to move around freely, gather/store items easily and prepare meals efficiently?

3. Do some rooms in your home sit empty, while others are in constant use?

4. Do you find yourself walking from room to room to accomplish tasks or interact with family members?

5. Can you easily transition from the inside of your house to your outdoor spaces?

6. Do you have usable, accessible, well-planned outdoor spaces you want to spend time in?

7. Does your home have dedicated spaces for fitness, office work, and hobbies?

8. Will you and your spouse have similar interests, work and hobbies during retirement?

9. Do you have comfortable guest spaces for visiting friends and family that provide adequate privacy?

10. Could some spaces, like laundry rooms, offices and master bedrooms be more conveniently located?

Photo Credit: Stacy Zarin Goldberg Photography

CHAPTER 8

Changing Needs, Smarter Design, Better Lifestyle

> " Design is not just what it looks like and feels like. Design is how it works. "
> - Steve Jobs

As empty nesters, what you need from your home will change. And your home will have to change to meet those needs, especially if you want to age in place. Today, as architect-builders, we are literally shaping homes to the specific needs and habits of our homeowners. We are breaking free from the cookie-cutter floor plans of planned communities and are transforming traditional designs into smarter spaces. This smart design approach not only makes for a safer, more efficient home as we move through retirement, it gives us the ability to greatly improve a homeowner's lifestyle today, as well as later in life. It focuses on function, but not at the expense of form. With smart design your home can be a beautiful everyday retreat, custom fit to your lifestyle while supporting your quality of life at any age. This thoughtful, deliberate and customized approach is at the heart of any successful plan for aging in place. This is nesting for empty nesters at its best.

 TIP: *Listen closely to the questions your architect-builder is asking you. A true aging in place professional will conduct a "home audit" by asking a lot of questions about your lifestyle and the way you use your house to create a home that suits your needs and your sense of style. If you're not getting a lot of questions from your building and remodeling professional, you may not be getting the home you need. Choose your aging in place professional wisely.*

CHAPTER 9

Do I Remodel, Move or Build New?

> " Some people look for a beautiful place. Others make a place beautiful. "
> – Hazrat Inayat Khan

To properly prepare your home for a simplified and elegant lifestyle in retirement, perhaps the most difficult decision comes first: deciding whether to remodel, move or build new. Several factors will impact this decision, some practical and others emotional. Practically speaking, your financial position, your current age and stage in life, and your willingness to sort, pack and move all of your belongings will heavily influence whether moving and/or building a new home is the right choice for you. Another practical question to answer is, "Does my current home even have the potential to support the lifestyle and quality of life that I'm looking for in retirement and beyond?" In other words, can you "see" your home in a different way? Could it be a good candidate for remodeling as part of your overall aging in place plan? For some families, no matter how empty the nest, none of the practical factors will even compare to the emotional ties they have to their current home, neighborhood and memories. Most individuals or couples who choose to age in place in their current home will likely require some form of renovation to transform their home into the retirement retreat that will serve their needs for the next 25 years or more.

 TIP: Often, cost will be a determining factor in whether or not to remodel or build new for retirement. If you have lived in your home for many years, you may be unfamiliar with current building and materials costs. Work with an architect-builder early in the process to assess your current home and create an estimate of what particular projects may cost. An informed choice is always easier to make!

39

Photo Credit:
Ali Rizvi Photography

CHAPTER 10

Building New for the New You – Considerations

> 66 For the most part things never get built the way they were drawn. 99
> - Maya Lin

B uilding a new home for your new life as an empty nester is an ambitious and exciting opportunity. There are many advantages to consider. Homeowners today have the widest variety of stylish and eco-friendly materials, finishes, and products designed specifically for aging in place or to accommodate any level of ability you or a family member may require in a custom built home. To take advantage of all of the latest trends, techniques and products available, we recommend working with an experienced architect-builder who can show you all of your options and bring your dream home to life. Working with a local architect-builder can also be helpful in selecting a site for your new home, as he or she likely knows the area well, including which lots may be available in the neighborhoods that are most conducive to aging in place. Neighborhoods that are most conducive to aging in place have easy access to transportation, retail stores, and medical care, as well as cultural and outdoor activities. Building new is a good option if you can make a large initial investment and have the time and patience to see your dream come to life from the ground up. Overall, building new can be less expensive per square foot, but requires a larger initial investment.

 TIP: If you decide to build new, choose an architect-builder familiar with the rapidly expanding array of Universal Design and "home for life" design features, products and trends. An experienced aging in place professional can help you budget wisely to incorporate the elements that will make the biggest impact on your plan for Vacation Style Living™.

CHAPTER 11

Remodeling for Retirement and Beyond

> 66 The most important work you will ever do will be within the walls of your own home. 99
> – Harold B. Lee

R eimagining your current home for retirement is also an exciting option and will be most attractive to the 87% of adults 65 and over who want to stay in their current home and community as they age. Remodeling to transform your current home into the retirement retreat that will best serve your needs in this season of life must start with a comprehensive strategy, a well thought out plan that starts with your unique combination of activities, hobbies, lifestyle, any necessary accommodations and your desired quality of life in mind. Remodeling done well will increase the overall value of your home giving you the peace of mind that you have made a wise investment. As mentioned, remodeling will require "seeing" your home in a new way and will require the skills of an experienced architect-builder. Some changes may be subtle, but others may be more extreme as your architect-builder removes walls, transforms kitchens and baths, and changes the use and purpose of spaces to give you the open, simplified, and luxurious dream home you've always wanted.

 TIP: Embrace "adaptable design" – the approach of building or remodeling a home to adapt to the needs of the homeowner over time. Framing and wiring can be anticipated and put in place for future upgrades to the areas that require the most adaptation as we age: hallways, doorways, bathrooms, kitchens, etc. This principle may also apply to your budget strategy, allowing you to phase in improvements as necessary and as affordable.

CHAPTER 12

Multi-Generational Living – Making Room for Mom & Dad

> " Give the ones you love wings to fly, roots to come back and reasons to stay. "
> – Dalai Lama

There's another kind of remodeling for aging in place that is becoming increasingly popular – building an addition to your existing home that serves as a comfortable main floor master suite for your parents. Many families are making multi-generational living part of their aging in place plan. There are many benefits to this approach. Families can spend more time together, but "mom and dad" can still maintain their privacy and independence by retreating into their own suite, which may include a master bedroom, a small open kitchen, a comfortable sitting area, a beautifully designed master bath, as well as access to a functional outdoor space like a patio or multi-use garden. This option is not only more cost effective when compared to the average fees for retirement communities or assisted living facilities, it also increases the square footage and overall value of your existing home. And the best bonus of all, your home is automatically transformed into a retirement-ready retreat of your design so you can easily age in place when it's your turn to become empty nesters. Making the most of this strategic approach will often require the experience and insight of a local architect who can help you maximize your space and your investment.

 TIP: Involving your parents in a frank discussion of some of the key design decisions as you prepare your home for multi-generational living can have many benefits. Aligning your vision for this added special space can ensure your older family members will have the functionality they need, the features they want, and make for happier housemates.

CHAPTER 13

"I just can't see it." –
When to Call in an Expert

> " An idea is salvation by imagination. "
> – Frank Lloyd Wright

You may be starting to get a vision of what your unique style of aging in place will look and feel like. You may already be envisioning a space that makes your day-to-day life easier, more comfortable and more stylish. You may even be looking forward to the friends and family who will love to visit you in your spacious, easy to use home complete with guest rooms and outdoor entertaining space. That may be a little easier with your eyes closed. But when you look around your existing home, can you see it transformed? Can you see a new configuration, a new flow, a new layout that will give you the lifestyle you're looking for right where you're standing? Do you know the trends and techniques that can transform your existing house into your dream home? If you can't "see" it, it's time to call an expert. Experienced architect-builders can see hidden potential and new opportunities simply by walking through your home. Whether you know exactly what you want or whether you aren't quite sure what to do, if you want to prepare your home for retirement and beyond it's time to call an architect who is knowledgeable about the most current approaches and designs for aging in place (a CAPS professional), knows your community and is committed to your vision for an enhanced lifestyle for many, many years to come. Let's get started.

 TIP: *The Certified Aging in Place Specialists (CAPS) program was developed by the National Association of Home Builders (NAHB) in collaboration with AARP. Both organizations offer a wealth of interesting and important aging in place information. You can find links to both organizations in the "Resources" section of this book.*

SECTION 2:

The Vacation Style Living™ Solution to Aging in Place

Photo Credit: Ali Rizvi Photography

Photo Credit: Ali Rizvi Photography

CHAPTER 14
What is Vacation Style Living™?

Vacation Style Living™ is a unique approach to home design created over 20 years of working with families to build or remodel the home of their dreams. A Vacation Style Living™ home considers every aspect of the home; the needs and activities of the family, the layout and use of space, the connection of the spaces inside and out, and the finishes and details that will make the house a custom-fit home that supports the entire family. The process starts with really listening to the homeowners, the family and their needs. While every Vacation Style Living™ home reflects the individual style and lifestyle of the family, there are several key components that are a part of every Vacation Style Living™ home that will be discussed in this section. By building the home around the family and the design process around these key components, homeowners can achieve the casual luxury lifestyle so many desire. While the Vacation Style Living™ approach can be applied to any home and any homeowners at any stage of life, it is critical to the success of any aging in place plan and can be your roadmap to retiring in comfort and style.

 TIP: As you prepare for life's ultimate vacation – retirement – keep a list of the features, fixtures, amenities, and feelings that made you want your vacations to never end. By incorporating some of these aspects of functionality and style into your home, you can begin to experience Vacation Style Living ™.

Photo Credit: Stacy Zarin Goldberg Photography

CHAPTER 15

What will I need? The Elements of a Vacation Style Living™ Home for Retirement

> **66** Have nothing in your house that you do not know to be useful, or believe to be. **99**
> – William Morris

A Vacation Style Home for retirement is designed with the style you love for the lifestyle you deserve. The Vacation Style Living™ approach to aging in place centers on main floor living, maximizing space and putting everything you need within comfortable – and beautiful – reach. It takes into consideration the spaces you use the most – for preparing healthy meals, entertaining friends and family, and working on your new business or hobby – and makes the most of them by reimagining your space and challenging the traditional approach to square footage. A great home for retirement focuses as much on functionality as it does on finishes. Open floor plans lead on to wider hallways and step-free entrances, while furniture, lighting and fixtures are carefully chosen for their resort-like feel and easy-to-use convenience. Outdoor spaces that flow naturally from the interior spaces are master-planned into the overall design instantly increasing the use, feel and "size" of your home. And all of it is inspired by what inspires you – a nest reimagined for the next great chapter of your life and custom-fit to your lifestyle.

 TIP: *Don't just think function – think fun! Preparing for Vacation Style Living™ can include zero-entry pools and showers, a main floor exercise or mindfulness space, a library with sufficient lighting and easy to access books. It's important to consider what you will need, but throw a few "wants" on the list, too.*

Photo Credit: Ali Rizvi Photography

Main Floor Living

> **" Space is the breath of art. "**
> **– Frank Lloyd Wright**

Main floor living is the mainstay of aging in place. As your nest empties, you can enjoy the ease of living on a single level with a master suite, eat in kitchen, living room, laundry, fitness area, office space, patio, deck and gardens all on the same level. No steps, no thresholds, fewer doors, and more room to move. With smart design, the rooms of your Vacation Style Living™ home relate to one another easily with a natural flow that maximizes space, while minimizing your effort to use it. For many, the biggest change will be adding a main level master suite or even a main floor guest suite. But for some that's just the beginning. Many couples as they design their Vacation Style Living™ home will choose his and hers master bathrooms with his and hers closets to match! Also on the main level, his and hers offices and hobby spaces are becoming more common. Formal dining rooms are giving way to larger, more convenient chef's kitchens with eat in dining areas better suited for casual family-style entertaining and daily living.

 TIP: *After making a lifetime of memories in your existing home, it may be difficult to "see" it in a new configuration. Ask an architect to walk through your home with you. They can often suggest options and point out opportunities to embrace main floor living that you may have missed.*

Photo Credit: Stacy Zarin Goldberg Photography

CHAPTER 17

Smarter Spaces: Where do you really "live"?

> " Simplicity is the ultimate sophistication. "
> – Leonardo Da Vinci

Where do you spend most of your time in your home? Where do you gather, relax and entertain? In other words, what is the hub of your home? For many it will be the kitchen, for others it's the family room and for still others it will be the outdoor spaces that flow easily from these rooms. The key to creating smarter spaces is identifying which rooms you really use, not just the rooms you think you're "supposed" to have or the rooms dictated by tradition. Smart design focuses on the rooms that are key to the daily lifestyle you are trying to achieve and builds the house around them. Sometimes the easiest way to identify the spaces you use the most is by looking at the spaces you rarely use at all: formal living room, formal dining room, oversized entryways, etc. What if you could have less of what you don't use and more space for the rooms you really live in? That's the Vacation Style Living™ lifestyle!

 TIP: There are often telltale signs that will help you determine which areas of your home need to shrink or be eliminated and which areas need to be bigger or more functional. Clutter is a key sign that a particular room doesn't provide enough functional storage or has become a dumping ground for everything and anything that won't fit easily into other high traffic rooms. Another clue is seating. Assess which chairs, couches, etc., haven't been used in weeks, months or years. This is a good sign that the room is wasted, underutilized space that could be reconfigured to serve you better.

CHAPTER 18

Finding Space and Maximizing Floor Plan

> ❝ Design is thinking made visual. ❞
> – Saul Bass

Building new or remodeling can give you the freedom to see through walls, to reimagine your traditional layout and start over by giving the rooms with the most use the most floor space. Is your kitchen cramped? Consider remodeling to eliminate your formal dining room and capture that square footage to expand your kitchen, add a butler's pantry or create the functional, convenient mudroom/laundry room you've always wanted. "Dead spaces" can come to life as attractive and efficient storage or display areas and choppy, boxy floor plans can be opened to create welcoming spaces with pleasant lines of sight. What seems impossible for the average homeowner may be a simple fix for a trained architect-builder. Moving windows, doors and walls can transform a home instantly, but are not do-it-yourself projects. By working with an experienced architect certified in the latest aging in place practices and techniques, you can master plan your retirement remodel and implement it all at once or phase it in over several years. It's your time. Do it your way.

 TIP: Cabinetry is offering more solutions than ever to make the most of your spaces. Think beyond just storage, to a conveniently located desk or task area, extra serving space for entertaining, or providing easy to reach covered storage for items you use often but don't want to keep on display.

CHAPTER 19

Does Size Really Matter?
A New Approach to Square Footage

> " The architect must get to know the people who will live in the planned house. From their needs, the rest inevitably follows. "
> - Ludwig Mies van der Rohe

As your nest empties you may find yourself living in a three-story colonial that fits your new lifestyle about as well as old stretched out sock. Homes in which the spaces you have versus the spaces you actually use are out of balance cause many empty nesters to assume it's time to downsize. But that's not always the case! Rather than downsize, "right size" to improve your lifestyle and accommodate your entire family. You can make your existing home fit like a glove again by taking a new approach to square footage. Most multi-level homes are built with roughly the same square footage on each level, but few people – especially empty nesters – spend an equal amount of time on each floor. By far, outside of sleeping, the main level of your home likely gets the most use. So rather than downsizing your house, upsize your main level! Additions to the main level put the proportions of your home into proper balance with the most space on the main level and less space on the upper and basement levels. Main floor living for aging in place can result in luxurious second floor guest suites for visiting family and friends. Basement spaces can be transformed into clean, convenient and efficient storage areas.

 TIP: *Optimizing your home for main floor living by expanding your main level will increase the value of your home by increasing the square footage and making it more attractive to future home buyers who will be looking for the Vacation Style Living™ lifestyle.*

CHAPTER 20

Vacation Style Living™ – The Basics of Vacation Style Aging in Place

> 66 Life should be chic, glamorous, and colorful – and so should your home. 99
> - Jonathan Adler

Time and time again we hear people in their own homes reminiscing about the hotel or resort they stayed in on vacation, "It was so open! So bright! We had everything we needed and it was just perfect. We could really live in a place like that!" And they're right! You can live in a place like that! Living like you're on vacation is at the heart of the Vacation Style Living™ approach – especially in retirement. Why spend only two weeks a year living the lifestyle of your dreams when you could transform your home into the vacation-style retreat you're always talking about? Shouldn't your home be the place you most want to be – living like you're on vacation 365 days a year? Isn't that the definition of retirement – an endless vacation? The luxury of vacation-style accommodations is the result of open concept living, quality fixtures and finishes, ease of movement, and the ability to relax and entertain in an environment that flows easily from indoors to outdoors. That is the Vacation Style Living™ approach to aging in place.

 TIP: *Ask yourself, what was it about a much loved resort or vacation rental that made life "feel so easy" in that space. Was it the simplicity of the furnishings, the layout, the convenient location of closets and amenities? These items should be at the top of your list when designing your Vacation Style Living™ home.*

Photo Credit: Galie Photography

CHAPTER 21

Find Inspiration

> **" An interior is the natural projection of the soul. "**
> **– Coco Chanel**

Starting the transformation of your home for retirement and beyond can be daunting. The best place to start is by finding what inspires you. That resort you stayed in, the vacation you loved, the photo from a catalog or magazine that you've memorized and daydreamed about. Pulling together these items or seeking out new sources of inspiration will help your architect create the retirement retreat of your dreams. Think outside of your walls and beyond your pre-conceived notions of what retirement would be or should be. Luxury is not limited by your budget, only by your thinking. Today, stylish quality fixtures, finishes and furnishings are available at a wide range of price points and, done well, can make any home feel like a five-star resort. Proper use of lighting and color can transform the ordinary to the extraordinary. But, by far, the most luxurious aspect of your home will be the space. An open, warm, welcoming space is luxury defined and will be one you and your friends and family will want to come home to again and again. So gather your inspiration, find an experienced professional and let your home become your dream come true.

 TIP: *Sometimes architectural inspiration doesn't come from architectural elements at all. A favorite painting, pillow, rug, movie or book that captures your eye and your imagination may be the right place to start. Building on a style, color scheme, or "feeling" you already love, whatever the inspiration, will help you – and your architect – translate that feeling to your entire Vacation Style Living™ home.*

Photo Credit: Stacy Zarin Goldberg Photography

CHAPTER 22
Choose a Style

> ❝ I'm going to make everything around me beautiful – that will be my life. ❞
> – Elsie de Wolfe

The style you ultimately choose for your new home – whether remodeled or new – will largely inform nearly every decision you make during the design process. Style shouldn't be an afterthought. Be it seaside cottage, mountain retreat, or elegant contemporary – your style should be reflected inside and out. Not only will a unified and well-implemented style make for a beautiful home, it will give the impression of being a larger home as the eye will flow effortlessly from one space to the next. Your style will impact not only the fixtures and finishes, but also the flooring, the trim and mouldings, the scale of the rooms and outdoor spaces, as well. A good architect-builder will work with you to help define your style and ensure that it is reflected in your new space. Many work closely with interior designers who can also assist you when making key décor and color choices.

 TIP: Color choices are critical, but can be overwhelming and difficult to make. Think about objects that help create the environment you are looking for. Warm, cozy homes can be created with a "cappuccino" color palette of caramel, cream, coffee bean and white. While a bright airy feel might best be captured by the colors found at the shore – sea glass, sand, sky and the many colors of the sea. Use everyday items to inspire your color and style choices and watch your customized Vacation Style Living™ home come to life.

Photo Credit: Stacy Zarin Goldberg Photography

CHAPTER 23
Lighting

The right lighting makes a house feel like a home. The wrong lighting – or lack of lighting – makes a house feel cold, stark and unfinished. Careful consideration of lighting for your Vacation Style Living™ home is a must. Lighting is one of the finest details in home design and can make or break the success of a remodel or build. Lighting falls into three categories; general, task and ambient lighting. General lighting may include recessed lights or overhead fixtures. Task lighting is trained on specific areas: pendants over a kitchen prep space or under cabinets, or adjustable reading sconces strategically placed at your bedside. When it comes to aging in place, sufficient general and task lighting are key for safety and ease of use. Ambient lighting will contribute largely to the style and overall feel of a home and is often used to balance or replace sometimes overpowering and unattractive overhead lighting. Just as your home remodel or build should be carefully master planned, so should the lighting. Well-planned lighting won't rely solely on dimmer switches and floor lamps to light a space or create a mood. When considering aging in place, light switches should be placed at a convenient height. In a Vacation Style Living™ home the right lighting will add a layer of luxury and the comfort of always having the right light for any task or gathering at your fingertips.

 TIP: Consider choosing fixtures that will allow for higher wattage bulbs to ensure you will always have sufficient light. Avoid fixtures and installations that create glare. Use night-lights and illuminate the keyhole on your main point of entry. And move light switches to be no higher than 48" from the floor.

Photo Credit: Stacy Zarin Goldberg Photography

CHAPTER 24
Interior Finishes

The details are not the details. They make the design.
– Charles Eames

nvesting in your future by remodeling or building the home that will take you through retirement and beyond gives you the rare opportunity to fully reimagine your experience by carefully choosing the finishes of your new home. Backsplashes, flooring, trim, paint, railings, drawer pulls, countertops, and cabinetry – the choices you make for the finishes of these items will largely dictate the look and feel of your home. Will it be deeply colored, warm and cozy? Or will it be light, bright and airy? The finishes, when combined with your lighting plan, will determine your home's personality, as much as your furnishings and layout. Experiment with contrasting finishes and textures; light and dark cabinetry or countertops in the same kitchen; smooth granite countertops with rough stacked stone backsplashes; pebbled tile in a shower playing off the straight lines of plank tiles on the bathroom walls and floor. Open your design mind to new possibilities, there are more available than ever before. Working closely with your architect-builder will help you make choices that stand the test of time in terms of durability and style.

 TIP: Finishes should be as functional as they are beautiful. Think non-slip tile in the shower, low pile or no-pile carpeting, easy to maintain surfaces, and high quality durable flooring that will stand the test of time.

Photo Credit: Francisca Alonso

CHAPTER 25

Hidden Hazards and Beautiful Solutions

> **On matters of style, swim with the current, on matters of principle, stand like a rock.**
> – Thomas Jefferson

Planning now to have a great quality of life in your own home in the decades to come largely depends on your home's ability to help you live a fulfilling life independently. To live independently and comfortably in our homes late into life requires a safe environment. The Vacation Style Living™ approach to aging in place includes assessing the potential hidden dangers in your home and replaces them with the wide variety of beautiful solutions available today. Hidden hazards in your home may include raised thresholds between rooms, shower entries with curbs to step over, sharp countertop corners and slick tile. Architects can show you fixtures and techniques designed for safety but disguised as elements of style. Beautiful non-skid tiles, stunning low-pile carpets, luxurious wide passageways and zero entry, doorless showers (featured here) are all options that will make day-to-day living beautifully easy and safe. Conveniently located, easy to reach rocker-style light switches, electrical outlets, window latches, sensor driven faucets, roll-away drawers, easy to reach thermostats, lever-style door handles, and remote controlled fans and fireplaces will all add to the comfortable life you crave.

 TIP: *New products designed specifically for stylish aging in place are coming to market every day. Home shows, design houses and architectural magazines and websites will help you stay abreast of the latest innovations. Read reviews and ask your architect if the new products deliver on their promises and are right for your Vacation Style Living™ home.*

Photo Credit: Stacy Zarin Goldberg Photography

CHAPTER 26
Furniture

> **" Your home should tell the story of who you are, and be a collection of what you love... "**
> **- Nate Berkus**

Furniture is a key ingredient in both the style and comfort of any home. It is often among the last items placed in a room, but should be one of the very first considerations. While the look and feel of furniture is important, the size is paramount and a good architect-builder will work with a homeowner to determine the key pieces that must be worked into the design of the home. Second only to overall layout, furnishings are at the key intersection of style and functionality. Pieces should "anchor" a room and help to define a style, but also afford the comfort and support the homeowners and their valued guests deserve. Do the grandchildren prefer to pile onto one couch to watch a movie? Are there friends and family who might prefer a firm chair that is as easy to get into as it is to get out of? Are there shaded and sun-loving furniture options in the outdoors spaces? And are there comfortable and functional seating and workspace pieces for business tasks, hobbies and online activities? All of these are important questions and your choices will greatly impact your aging in place quality of life for both you and your guests.

 TIP: *If you plan to include a key piece of furniture in your design or a must-have couch in your new main floor configuration, share the dimensions, use and preferred placement of the piece with your architect. Rooms can be "built around" specific needs, uses and even furniture.*

CHAPTER 27

Elements to Eliminate

> **" Architecture begins where engineering ends. "**
> **– Walter Gropius**

When building a new home or remodeling your existing home into a home for life, it's a good idea to start with his and hers lists of must haves to help your architect create a design that is custom fit to your lifestyle. In addition, an aging in place certified architect will also have a list for you – a list of must not haves, the items that must be eliminated in a home designed for independent living. That list includes:

- Sunken living rooms
- Unnecessary steps and stairs
- Narrow halls and doorways
- Step in baths or showers
- Poor lighting

 TIP: *The key to staying in your Vacation Style Living™ home for many years to come is thinking ahead. What works today, may not work tomorrow. Plan ahead for a life of ease, beauty and functionality by eliminating potential hazards now and building in features that will serve you well 20 years down the road.*

Photo Credit: Stacy Zarin Goldberg Photography

CHAPTER 28

It's All About the Flow – Connecting Inside with Outside

> **In Japanese houses the interior melts into the garden of the outside world.**
> – Stephan Gardiner

The way a home functions – or doesn't – also impacts how it feels. A home in which the rooms connect awkwardly or inefficiently will feel boxy, chopped up, even smaller regardless of its square footage. Similarly, if your home is master planned with flow in mind, even a small house will seem larger, more comfortable and generally a more pleasant place to be. Flow is how one space connects to another and it is also a key component of a Vacation Style Living™ home. It's a critical consideration when designing for aging in place as rooms need to be easy to access and conveniently placed. If, as suggested, you embrace open concept main floor living, flow can add visual interest to a centralized space that leads off to other areas of the house. A common mistake is failing to consider flow between your indoor and outdoor spaces. A home should flow easily from the front door through to the main area of the home and out into the outdoor spaces at the back of the house. You can easily achieve indoor/outdoor flow by using similar materials and finishes inside and out. If the interior hardwood is laid perpendicular to the deck door, the deck flooring should carry on in the same direction such that the flooring seems to "flow" from one space to the other. A stone portico could flow into a foyer and living room that feature the same or similar stone on the fireplace. By unifying these elements and planning for flow, your home will feel larger, more welcoming and more like a luxury retreat - your own personal resort!

 TIP: *Updating the size and placement of windows and doors can completely transform the flow and feel of your home. An architect can tell you what's possible within your home and your budget when considering moving and expanding windows and doors.*

CHAPTER 29

Outdoor Spaces

> **Don't divide architecture, landscape and gardening; to me they are one.**
> **– Luis Barragan**

Outdoor spaces are as much a part of your home as the indoor spaces and should be treated that way. Planning for and carefully designing your outdoor spaces can double the livable space of your home and allow you to really enjoy everything your home has to offer. First, determine which types of outdoor spaces you would like to have and how you plan to use them – a deck for entertaining, a pool for exercise and lounging, a vegetable or flower garden, a separate patio for grilling, a play area for grandchildren, etc. Then, it's all about the flow. How can you easily access those outdoor "rooms" from your indoor rooms and where is the most logical location for each outdoor space? For example, a grilling patio may make the most sense located just off the kitchen, while the deck would flow nicely from the living room or open concept area for entertaining. Similarly, the zero entry pool should have access to the master bedroom or an area of the house that leads to a shower and changing room. A garden with access to both the mudroom and the garage would provide easy access to tools, a sink for rinsing fresh produce and a place to remove muddy gardening shoes and gloves. Make sure to maximize the placement of your beautiful flower garden such that it can be seen from other indoor and outdoor rooms of your home. The planning of outdoor spaces also applies to entrances and approaches and care should be taken to make entries and walkways step free, welcoming and easily "visitable" for your guests of all ages.

 TIP: *Keep in mind that even though you can phase in the creation of your outdoor spaces, they should be part of your aging in place master plan from the start. Your architect-builder and their landscape architect can work with you to make these spaces a favorite component of your retirement lifestyle.*

Photo Credit:
Bob Narod, Photographer

CHAPTER 30
Exterior Finishes

> 66 **The sun never knew how great it was until it hit the side of a building.** 99
> – Louis Khan

Using smart design to choose exterior finishes can add style and personality to your home, but will also let you determine the level of maintenance you want to tackle in retirement and beyond. High style, low maintenance options abound. Exterior finishes like siding, window casings, railings, masonry and fixtures are being designed with longevity, maintenance and weather resistance in mind. While it's important to design your exterior to reflect your style and look good from all sides, the front elevation and entrance are key. Remodeling the entryway of your home to age in place doesn't mean obtrusive ramps that look like an awkward afterthought. In many cases your architect can redesign a step-free approach to your home that is well-lit, complements the style of your home and flows easily to your front door. If you are transitioning to main floor living or if you are adding a main floor in-law suite by building an addition to your existing home, choosing the right exterior finishes can make the house appear more homogenous. Using consistent doors, windows, lighting, trim and exterior materials, color and landscaping will make your addition appear original to the home. Take this opportunity to give the roof a facelift and a consistent layer of new shingles will tie the new and existing elements of your home together, as well.

 TIP: *Exterior finishes are no place to skimp as they must hold up to the elements. Choose high quality, low maintenance exterior finishes that have a proven track record of durability.*

Getting Started

" If you think good design is expensive, you should look at bad design. "
- Dr. Ralf Speth

Photo Credit: Stacy Zarin Goldberg Photography

CHAPTER 31
Choosing an Architect

> " Since future generations and other living species depend on us,
> we must acknowledge that the Earth does not belong to us,
> but that we belong to the Earth. "
> - Melvin Villarroel Roldan

C hoosing an architect to help make your dream home a reality is critical to the success of your project. It is even more important when you are designing or remodeling for aging in place. Start by finding an experienced architect-builder in your area with a CAPS designation. Certified Aging in Place Specialists (CAPS) architects have been trained in Universal Design – products and layouts that are usable by most people regardless of age or ability without the need for retrofitting. They know where to look for hidden dangers in your home and how to correct them. They also are aware of the specifications, modifications, and products necessary to make your home a safe, comfortable and attractive retirement retreat that will serve you well for decades to come. Your architect should be familiar with and have experience in designing the style of home or remodel you are considering. They should also be familiar with local permitting and inspection requirements, have a strong team of local tradesmen, and have solid relationships with vendors that are in good standing. References and examples of recent work designed for aging in place or universal design are a must. When remodeling, a good architect will ask to see your home early in the process.

 TIP: Remember, this person is more than the architect of your home, he or she is also the architect of your future in that home. You are choosing and trusting a professional who will greatly impact your quality of life in retirement. Choose carefully and choose well!

Photo Credit: Stacy Zarin Goldberg Photography

CHAPTER 32
What is an Architect-Builder?

" The difference between a builder and an architect is that an architect also cares about desire, about dreams. "
- Renzo Piano

An architect-builder is a valuable hybrid in the home building and remodeling industry. Traditionally, an architect designs the project with the budget, dreams and desires of the homeowners in mind. Their motivation is design and function. Builders are charged with bringing that project to life. Their motivation is staying within budget, delivering on time and meeting or exceeding local permitting and inspection requirements while meeting client expectations. An architect-builder, however, approaches a project from every angle and every step along the way. A Vacation Style Living™ architect-builder takes a holistic approach that results in a dream home for the family and brings that design to life within the family's budget and timeline with great quality and workmanship. An architect-builder simplifies the homebuilding and remodeling process, gives you a single point of contact for easy and open communication, and is a well-informed and experienced ally as you tackle one of the most important home projects of your lifetime – Nesting for Empty Nesters®, preparing your home for retirement and living a long and independent life in your expertly transformed vacation-style retreat. An architect-builder is your solution for preparing to age in place successfully.

 TIP: *Choosing an architect-builder ensures you do not sacrifice design to meet the budget and don't sacrifice the budget to preserve the design.*

Photo Credit: Bob Narod, Photographer

CHAPTER 33

Interviewing Your Architect-Builder

> " The dialogue between client and architect is about as intimate as any conversation you can have, because when you're talking about building a house, you're talking about dreams. "
> - Robert A. M. Stern

Choosing an architect starts with asking good questions, like:

1. Do you have a portfolio of your projects that I may review?
2. Do you have a list of references I may contact?
3. What kind of training have you had?
4. Do you have a CAPS Certification and are you familiar with Universal Design?
5. How long have you been an architect-builder?
6. How long have you been building and remodeling homes in our area?
7. What is your design philosophy?
8. How do you work? What is the process for engaging on a project?
9. What is your project management process like?
10. How often can I expect to hear from you with updates during the project?

If you like what you see and hear, the next question should be an enthusiastic, "When can we get started?!"

 TIP: *If a potential architect is reticent to answer your questions, keep looking! This is a key indicator of how a professional will work with you during the critical planning and construction phases.*

CHAPTER 34

Budgeting: How to Age in Place without Breaking the Bank

> 66 Buy the best, and you'll cry only once. 99
> – Miles Redd

Every family, every home and every budget are different. But three key concepts apply to every home build or remodel:

1. Master Planning - Plan for your entire project from the start. Developing a Master Plan for your Vacation Style Living™ home is the most cost effective way to design your future. Elements of your plan can be phased in over time, but a Master Plan will save you in costly backtracks, afterthoughts and do overs.

2. Ask an Architect – For a fraction of the price of your entire build or remodel, you can engage an architect-builder at the beginning of your project to ensure that you are making sound design choices, maximizing your home's potential and value, and avoiding costly mistakes.

3. Build with Quality – The most expensive materials are the ones that need to be replaced! Your Vacation Style Living™ home is designed to serve you and make your best years beautiful, functional and easy. Choose high quality, low maintenance materials (and professionals) and you will save in the long run.

 TIP: *There are several types of financing to consider when building or remodeling your home for aging in place: Home equity lines of credit, a new mortgage, reverse mortgage funding, installment loans and credit cards. Always consult with your architect and your financial advisor to learn which budget and financing solutions are available and appropriate for your family.*

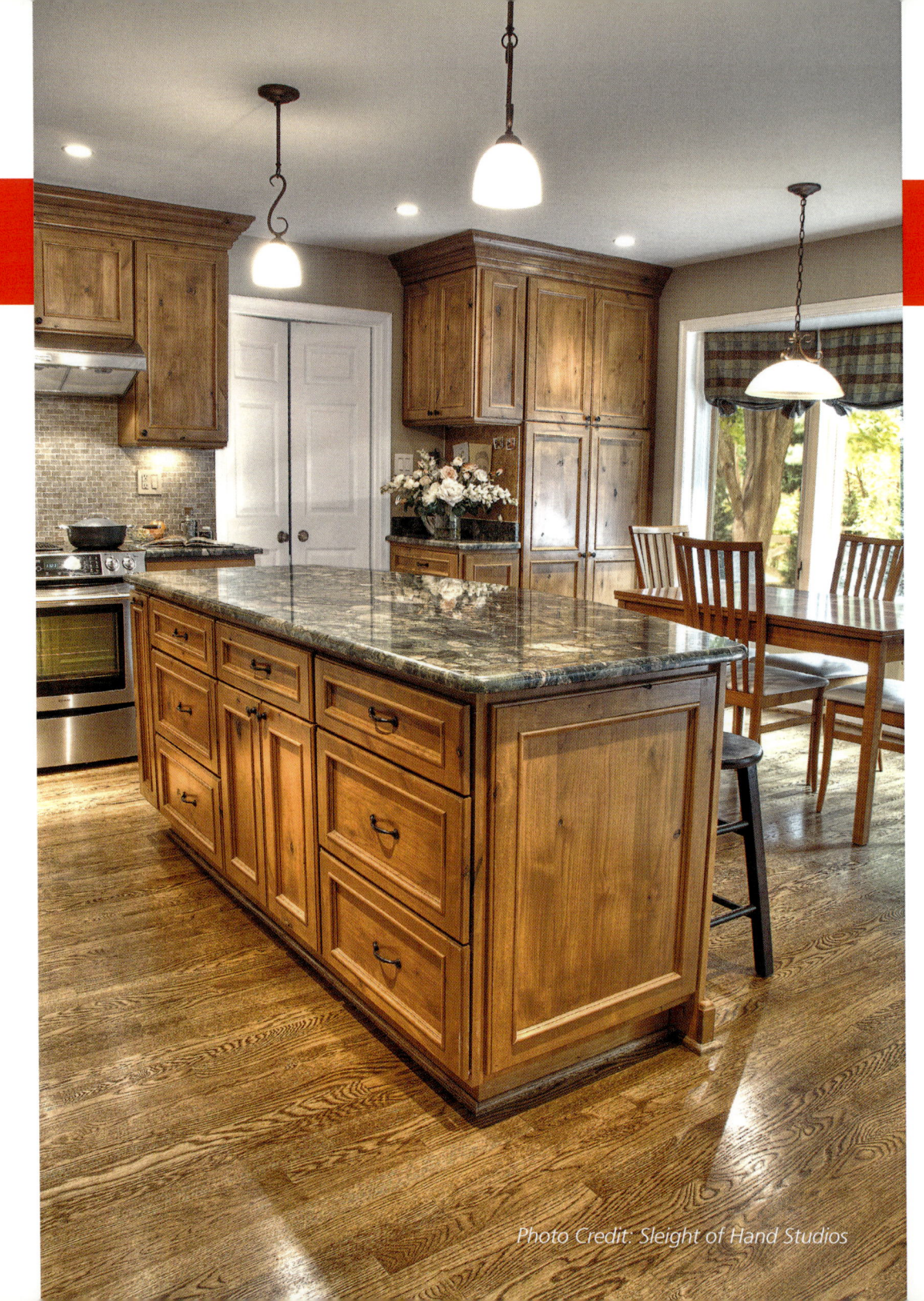

Photo Credit: Sleight of Hand Studios

CHAPTER 35

Start Now

> 66 Grow old along with me, the best is yet to be. 99
> – Browning

So, after reviewing the Vacation Style Living™ approach to aging in place, do you feel your home is ready to provide you the convenience, comfort, luxury, entertaining and family friendly, vacation-style retreat for the lifestyle you want in retirement and beyond? Surprisingly, statistics show that most people feel their current home is well equipped to handle aging in place and don't feel the need to start preparing for this important season of life. It's understandable. Baby Boomers are more active and productive than ever and may find it easier to deny what we know about the importance of nesting for empty nesters. Older respondents may want to delay a remodel or the acceptance that their beloved home no longer suits their needs as it is. The wisest homeowners today are the planners. Your ability to live a long, comfortable, simplified vacation-like lifestyle in your own home is a direct result of your pre-planning for aging in place. With the Vacation Style Living™ approach to aging in place, the future is yours to live in style, independently, enjoying the company of friends and family in your custom fit retirement retreat. It's never too early to start planning. Contact your local Certified Aging in Place (CAPS) architect-builder and start designing your future today!

 TIP: *Start master planning now. It's never too early to plan for Vacation Style Living™.*

Photo Credit: Bob Narod, Photographer

Francisca Alonso

Francisca Alonso has been designing, remodeling and building homes for families in the Northern Virginia area for more than 15 years as CEO and Co-Founder of AV Architects + Builders, established in 2001 and headquartered in Great Falls, VA. With a passion for building homes that are designed around a family's needs, she uses her Vacation Style Living™ approach to improve her clients' quality of life with a clever combination of casual luxury and practical conveniences for every stage of life. An area builder of choice, Alonso has assembled a skilled team of experienced craftsmen to execute her designs with excellence, whether bringing a client's dream home to life or partnering with area colleagues to ensure their architectural vision is achieved on time, on budget and above expectations. A magna cum laude graduate of The School of Architecture at The Catholic University, Alonso is also CAPS Certified. Born in Chile and raised in Spain, she comes from a family of architects and builders including her father, internationally acclaimed luxury resort designer and architect Melvin Villarroel Roldan. Alonso and her husband, fellow architect, co-author and business partner Antonio Alonso, reside in Northern Virginia with their four teenage children.

Photo Credit: Ali Rizvi Photography

Antonio Alonso

Antonio Alonso, AIA, obtained his Bachelors of Science Degree from the prestigious Catholic University of America's School of Architecture and Planning. His background includes a wide range of experience in design and construction. While in architecture school, Antonio worked on the construction team building Washington's National Cathedral, gaining valuable experience in the field of construction.

Antonio has a reputation as a leader in developing pioneering concepts in architectural design and construction. This experience has translated into his passion for residential architectural design and construction and the belief in delivering high quality projects by integrating design and construction.

Antonio brings 25 years of diverse experience to AV Architects + Builders as Co-Founder and Vice President. His early involvement in the Master Planning of projects ensures that the design has a foundation for success.

RESOURCES

The following websites contain additional helpful information on Vacation Style Living™, aging in place and Universal Design:

AV Architects + Builders - www.avarchitectsbuild.com

AIA – The American Institute of Architects - http://network.aia.org/designforaging/home

National Association of Home Builders Certified Aging in Place Specialists - www.nahb.org/caps

The IDeA - Center for Inclusive Design and Environmental Access - http://idea.ap.buffalo.edu/

AARP - http://blog.aarp.org/category/livable-communities/

National Aging in Place Council - www.naipc.org

American Society on Aging - www.asaging.org